Drawn to Extinction

poems by

Carrie Hohmann Campbell

Finishing Line Press
Georgetown, Kentucky

Drawn to Extinction

Copyright © 2018 by Carrie Hohmann Campbell
ISBN 978-1-63534-477-6 First Edition
All rights reserved under International and Pan-American Copyright Conventions. No part of this book may be reproduced in any manner whatsoever without written permission from the publisher, except in the case of brief quotations embodied in critical articles and reviews.

ACKNOWLEDGMENTS

Grateful acknowledgement is made to the editorial staff of the following publications in which versions of these poems first appeared:

The Allegheny Review: "I have yet to answer anyone's questions"
The Bridge Literary Journal: "I don't want a dead bat on my conscience"
First Class Lit: "Hearing a name like yours too many times in one day"
H_NGM_N: "I used love like a scapegoat too" and "When you asked me if my dinner selection was a secret"
The Mackinac: "Hold your horses Cowboy"
Print Oriented Bastards: "Sometimes I want to be a catfish"
Sixth Finch: "Some things in the kitchen become metaphors"
Toad: "Altoona is stealing all our good stuff" and "January isn't a beginning"

Publisher: Leah Maines
Editor: Christen Kincaid
Cover Art and Design: Carrie Hohmann Campbell
Author Photo: Ashley Biltz Photography, www.ashleybiltzphotography.com

Printed in the USA on acid-free paper.
Order online: www.finishinglinepress.com
also available on amazon.com

Author inquiries and mail orders:
Finishing Line Press
P. O. Box 1626
Georgetown, Kentucky 40324
U. S. A.

Table of Contents

Lines

I.
Some Things in the Kitchen Become Metaphors 1
Hold Your Horses Cowboy 2
Altoona is Stealing All Our Good Stuff 3
Bread will never attack your brain again 4
That's Why We Call a Steak *Rare*,
    Because it's Eager 5
Since we've made "good morning" a verb 6
To Believe in Plurals 7

II.
Too Bad Word Bubbles are Only Found in Comics 10
Sometimes I Want to be a Catfish too 11
When You Asked if My Dinner Selection
    was a Secret 12
Drawn to Extinction 13
By March the Lake was Still Solid Enough
    to Walk on 14

III.
I Have Yet to Answer Anyone's Questions 16
Everything Makes Scents 17
Desire is an Acid Rain 18
I Use Love Like a Scapegoat too 19
Hearing a Name Like Yours too Many Times
    in One Day 20
Bad Weather in the Midwest 21
I Don't Want a Dead Bat on My Conscience 22
January Isn't a Beginning 23

for Jake

> "The heart lies to itself because it must."
>
> JACK GILBERT

Lines

I believe less and less in spaces
       between bodies that never touch.
Show me hands that promise not to leave
          and a rhetoric I don't want to refuse.
    When he tells me there is nothing else on Earth
           like a gunshot
that marks such a clear line
      between the way things were and the way they are now,
I can't help thinking
         how relationships between people are like that
      and how those are anything but clear—
       an explosive existence, the trajectory
    with too many landing points.
I want to believe in fate
            but desire alone won't create holes.

I.

Some Things in the Kitchen Become Metaphors

Would it be bad if I said I was the owl
    pepper-shaker before I met you, since it was (still
        is) empty and now I've moved up to the
            salt-shaker (full of white squares, but
      still an owl) Maybe it's not that at
          all and we just have a full
                set or I am hungry enough
            to think in salt-shakers

  This is the type of thing
      that makes me careless and multiplies the little lion inside
          its ribbed cage, since I'm scared
    to have something to lose, but here
          is that boot again, so I will just tell you
                to read Shakespeare's 43rd and wait
            for the second one to fall or the fourth or even
                        the nineteenth

I should tell you people become an idée fixe to me and I question
    your existence even when my ear
                  is pressed against a box containing
      what appears to be sounds you make
            We have been on fast-forward from the start
                Don't let go now: think of the landscapes we
                        can cover

Hold Your Horses Cowboy

If I had this *in the bag* then you'd be in
        a brown paper one from the state store,
waiting for me to turn around, take off
        *the whole kit and cabood*le so I could
            get your dander up and *jump the gun.*

I call things like I see 'em and how I see
things: teal eyes, tan boots, and a face
        that's forgotten the purpose of a razor,
            are only half. There's no substitute
                for you, McCoy—so, *let's paint this town*
    its favorite color,
        and see how long it takes for the satellites
to update their pixels before we go
        back to the drawing board, this time
    give it a real *shot in the arm.*

Altoona is Stealing All of Our Good Stuff

It started with our area code, then moved on to the waffle iron,
    and ultimately the reservoirs were emptied,
        Brody's was left to dust mites and the train whistles stopped.
    Pittsburgh doesn't have to worry you say.

Did it ever really have to? I wonder. Nothing good can come of this;
    just more boxes filled with my things and nowhere to stack them.

It seems like everything's more complicated nowadays, even stasis.

    Breathing's almost the same you say.
I wish I knew then how many others would go missing; I'd have stolen things
        or at least written them on the ledger.

Sometimes you have to take things for what they are you say.
    Sometimes I want to be a catfish I reply.

BREAD WILL NEVER ATTACK YOUR BRAIN AGAIN

if you cut it completely from your diet. Donuts
and macaroni and cheese must go too.
These are the types of things one thinks about
on the 2 train to Fulton. All those pockets
for jam or peanut butter sink into the accordion folds.
I need to stop eating it around you; the aftermath
leaves me craving more than baguette.
There is a better substitute for flour and yeast
and all that kneading. The only way to know
for sure is to show you; give me your hands.

That's Why We Call a Steak *Rare*, Because it's Eager

One whiskey is all it takes to loosen my spine
        and call you *cowboy*
                A bar is a most public place
            and after a long week and those arms,
      I'm ready to get the hell out of here

It's nights like this that summer really thrives;
        clothes should be optional
              since it's too hot even for skin
        I don't care that our hands are sweaty
                or that what we have is on microwave;

I'm just thankful you tell them you've stopped
        looking I can feel the urgency in your words
            It's hard not to agree with you when you shout
                over the music: *Maybe we should get out of here*
            before we stick our hands anywhere crazy

Since We've Made "Good Morning" a Verb

I want to invent an entire language
      with you, keep the taste of your name in my mouth.
I haven't been able to wash off the grin.
My skin has static cling, a letter restored
      to my alphabet. You daydream
           at work and your hands fidget with the laser
    cutting out uneven metal strips, disappointed
the lines are not the contours of our bodies
               in the pale light before noon. It's scary
to think of how much doesn't get checked off
        the to-do list or whatever else I'm neglecting.
    If everyone acted like this we'd eventually starve.

To Believe in Plurals

There's not any good reason why
    I shouldn't believe people
    when they give me a compliment.
When I saw you for the first time,
    all I could do was stare since
        my tongue glued my entire mouth shut.
    Somewhere along the way I learned
to use words from my interior mumble
    and now every time I see green,
    your name scrolls across these eyes
        like a marquee. But the skeptic's still curious—
        Is it strange to believe in plurals?
    The gravel in your voice
        has my wires juiced at speeds
        even hummingbirds can't comprehend.

II.

Too Bad Word Bubbles Only Occur in Comics

You told me once *facetiously* has all
    the vowels as they appear
        in the alphabet plus a bonus of *y*.
    I collect these like squirrels
        hoard nuts, but for a purpose
    other than sustenance; I need to know
    who you are so I can decide what to do with you

Chickadees like most other birds have more
    than one song you say—I don't know
        what to make of this so I tell you my favorite part
    of a sonata is the recapitulation

There are things that remind me of a place I know
    nothing about and a bet I was willing to lose
        but that doesn't bring up the sun anymore
    than a voice heard on a screen means I can feel your skin
I want you to wake each morning to find my name
    hung on your lips, the remedy within sight.

Sometimes I want to be a Catfish

I say this
    like it's the only reasonable answer

or maybe it's because I've heard it before
    and it makes complete
        sense to be a catfish in a world filled with cod.

I want to keep you on your toes
so you'll do the same with me—

    not in the sense that we are blindly groping about
        with large philosophical hands or strange mannerisms,
but more like building a step-pyramid—

    so that by the time we make it to the top, there is nowhere
left to go but inside one another.

When You Asked Me if My Dinner Selection was a Secret

In recent months I have questioned many clocks

    and never once found

    the answer to an empty bed. Adequate

is a word that can sound perfectly emotionless but can serve

as a raincoat. I haven't tried very hard

    to make this work. I don't even know

    if the things I make up

are better than the ones that actually happen.

I don't even look at you : I am filled with a foaming soap.

There are cravings that include

    horizontal lines   hands   a clear night sky   red

    For once there are too many

    silent frames, too many holes to fill.

    For once these arms will remain stationary.

Drawn to Extinction

Without the certainty a name is supposed to give,

    I am drawn to my own extinction.

There is no panacea for my cardinal humor;

    I am *frantic for resolution*

    as one scar eventually outweighs the one before.

I cannot enjoy doing nothing

    when inside my head is the irregular

        heartbeat of our future;

    and even as your gradient is zero,

you mirror the same whimsy

    of our weather—

        hot then cold, with a dampness

    that exists because it can.

It is selfish to tell secrets;

        sometimes it can be quite stupid.

By March the Lake was Still Solid Enough to Walk on

It was here, between wormwood cherry walls covered in paper snowflakes,
    with a slanting bedroom floor, the tiny bed, antique lamp,
        the space heater that couldn't do a better job than a naked body—
                that you called me a siren.

You wanted me to roll your body into the lake and trap you in ice,
    if it meant spring would pass us by,
but the ducks came back a month later.
        The spring peepers let us know

the maple season was over,
    that we'd have to sustain ourselves beyond winter.
We buried a harmonica deep within the dark purple muscles
    of ribs and matchsticks in the small knot
        behind the left ear. We never were the ice

    or the metal skate indenting surface but the heat between them—
        ten molecular diameters thick.

III.

I Have Yet to Answer Anyone's Questions

On the surface it's like we never existed—
    I woke up today with no physical evidence:
        no tattoo, no dying flowers, no borrowed books,
        not even a typed word of emotion to use as proof.

The exterior is clean: your hand became a ghost, and your name's not
    spoken, the syllable used sparingly. In the mirror
        my eyes are where I left them;
        I can fool everyone

    except memory, who holds a scroll
        of bad jokes and the red vans of our childhoods.

Everything Makes Scents

From a young age you learn
    the difference between
        the good and the bad

    Paste smells good because you aren't
        supposed to eat it which fuels allegorical desires
            of forbidden fruit
Vanilla extract is a similar disappointment
    though bitter when tasted

Crayons have a collective scent
    which, like garlic, becomes better
      when broken
            You can't say that about too many
    things since most broken anythings
      are like skunks and electric fences—
        silent then gut-wrenching—
      the faint aftermath numbs everything

These things stay with you
    If they happen too early
        raised white lines, apprehension remain

Desire is an Acid Rain

You never wanted me like I wanted you—
    the way an ocean never
        leaves the shore,
            the way schoolchildren
always want to be first.

Tear off my wings
    and I grow
    feet. Throw salt in my eyes
        and I listen
for sunrise. There is nothing
        you can take I can't replace.

Use ropes to tie me to a bridge—
    I crack like an egg and run
        into the river;
    you will never know where I begin
        and if you have captured enough.

I Use Love Like a Scapegoat Too

If my mornings started out with Russian roulette
    I might actually do more with them

Hemingway said something about
    the loneliness that surfaces
after each wasted day

    I don't know how
to get my imagination
    back Star stickers cling

to my knee
    from tea this morning

    I had the perfect opportunity
to slap someone yesterday; I didn't take it

Maybe I'll finally get over you with all this
    good weather
I want to fill these envelopes
        with hornets, mail them to you

Hearing a Name Like Yours Too Many Times in One Day

If you want to come back I'd let you
       and I'd peel you
              from the wreck and dress you like an Egyptian
mummy. I'd bathe you
       in oatmeal and lemon wedges until you heal,

until I can feel rekindled bone
       and you tell me
            it hurts worse than light,
            worse than being broken

into particles and stretched
       across planets made of nitrogen gas,
       where if you had eyes
              they would disintegrate into tiny fires.

Bad Weather in the Midwest

When the radio announced

bad weather today, I imagined

    all the types you'd seen, were certainly

        driving through now.

    We were always incongruent,

    but the shrapnel still persists

      from an earlier winter. Separating words wrapped

around your wrist from something I love

    has become a masterful act of physics.

There will never be a second golden age

      and it's an empty gesture to say I felt

        too much of the wrong kinds of things,

      expecting to create something

          tangible from too few pieces.

Recently, I have found a rhythm compatible with life,

      but your memory—a cursory illusion—remains.

I Don't Want a Dead Bat on My Conscience

so I scoop him into a paper bag,
        fold the top over and staple
                the flap shut to give it some room,
            but not enough to escape.

Seeing the brown body, no bigger than a chicken egg,
    I can't think of you any longer,
        but focus on its breathing and my initial panic,
           frantic to keep it still, because I don't know
                what to do next. It's not fair
that the buzzing—a noise I'm sure meant fear
        and annoyance—
    is the same as a bee's,
        made me think of the nest we found in your garden,

how they floated from the ground,
        even after we had run indoors. I don't need
            to be stung again; I only want your eyes.

January Isn't a Beginning

Because it is the most familiar place I know,
I curl into the shape of the first letter of my name.

Desire always exceeds its object
and the wave fills in the space it left behind.

I want to stop writing your name
and sitting in the sand is only half the solution.

I am sick of not understanding my own language.
Blue is my favorite color and your eyes.

My life felt over, but wasn't.
It rained and snowed

at exactly the same moment.
I was set free by a mean wind

and I don't believe you'll remember this
in ten years. Everything that has stopped

growing will start growing again soon.
January isn't a beginning but a continuation

of what came before. Idioms like *everything
happens for a reason* were made up for people like me.

Notes

"Bread Will Never Attack Your Brain Again" lifts its title from an episode of *30 Rock*.

"Drawn to Extinction" borrows a phrase from Maggie Nelson's *The Argonauts*.

"I Use Love Like a Scapegoat Too" owes its title to a J. W. Lichtenberg poem of a similar name.

"January Isn't a Beginning" borrows a line from Maggie Nelson's poem "The Canal Diaries".

Additional Acknowledgments

Thank you to the faculty and students of the MFA program at New York University whose suggestions helped improve several of these poems and inspire several others.

Thank you to Christopher Bakken, Robert Bernard Hass, and Matthew Rohrer for their kind words and continued support of my writing.

To my many friends and teachers for their conversations and comments, especially Sarah Sala and Norm Milliken. And thanks to Nicholas Hess for letting me borrow a compass from his lovely cache of oddities to photograph for the cover.

And to my parents who've always encouraged my creative endeavors, and my sister. And, finally, to Jake Campbell whose continued support of my literary habits gives me courage, and Everett who has expanded the definition of love—thank you.

CARRIE HOHMANN CAMPBELL holds degrees from Allegheny College and New York University, where she taught as a Goldwater Hospital Fellow. She is the author of the chapbook *incongruent: someday* (dancing girl press, 2014) and teaches composition and creative writing at Edinboro University of Pennsylvania. She lives in northwestern Pennsylvania on a 10-acre farm with her husband and son. Visit her online at www.carriehohmanncampbell.com.

www.ingramcontent.com/pod-product-compliance
Lightning Source LLC
LaVergne TN
LVHW041600070426
835507LV00011B/1212